Deb Haaland

CHERRY LAKE PRESS

Published in the United States of America by Cherry Lake Publishing Group
Ann Arbor, Michigan
www.cherrylakepublishing.com

Reading Adviser: Beth Walker Gambro, MS, Ed., Reading Consultant, Yorkville, IL
Book Designer: Jennifer Wahi
Illustrator: Jeff Bane

Photo Credits: © a. v. ley/Shutterstock, 5; © LightField Studios/Shutterstock, 7; © Kit Leong/Shutterstock, 9; © All a Shutter/Shutterstock, 11, 22; © AFGE/flickr, 13; © Barbara Ash/Shutterstock, 15; © Clerk United States House of Representatives, 17, 23; © Romie Miller/Shutterstock, 19, 21; Jeff Bane, Cover, 1, 8, 10, 16; Various frames throughout, Shutterstock images

Cherry Lake Press is an imprint of Cherry Lake Publishing Group.

Library of Congress Cataloging-in-Publication Data

Names: Thiele, June, author. | Bane, Jeff, 1957- illustrator.
Title: Deb Haaland / by June Thiele ; illustrated by Jeff Bane.
Description: Ann Arbor, Michigan : Cherry Lake Publishing Group, [2022] | Series: My itty-bitty bio | Includes bibliographical references and index. | Audience: Grades K-1
Identifiers: LCCN 2021036529 (print) | LCCN 2021036530 (ebook) | ISBN 9781534198913 (hardcover) | ISBN 9781668900055 (paperback) | ISBN 9781668901496 (pdf) | ISBN 9781668905814 (ebook)
Subjects: LCSH: Haaland, Debra A., 1960---Juvenile literature. | United States. Congress. House--Biography--Juvenile literature. | Women legislators--United States--Biography--Juvenile literature. | Indian legislators--United States--Biography--Juvenile literature. | Legislators--United States--Biography--Juvenile literature. | Pueblo women--Biography--Juvenile literature. | Pueblo Indians--Biography--Juvenile literature. | New Mexico--Biography--Juvenile literature.
Classification: LCC E901.1.H33 T47 2022 (print) | LCC E901.1.H33 (ebook) | DDC 328.73/092 [B]--dc23
LC record available at https://lccn.loc.gov/2021036529
LC ebook record available at https://lccn.loc.gov/2021036530

Printed in the United States of America
Corporate Graphics

table of contents

My Story 4

Timeline 22

Glossary 24

Index 24

About the author: June Thiele writes and acts in Chicago where they live with their wife and child. June is Dena'ina Athabascan and Yup'ik, Indigenous cultures of Alaska. They try to get back home to Alaska as much as possible.

About the illustrator: Jeff Bane and his two business partners own a studio along the American River in Folsom, California, home of the 1849 Gold Rush. When Jeff's not sketching or illustrating for clients, he's either swimming or kayaking in the river to relax.

I was born in Arizona in 1960. I grew up with three sisters and one brother. We moved to New Mexico. We're **Indigenous**. We're **Laguna Pueblo**.

My parents were both in the **military**. We moved around a lot. I went to 13 different schools!

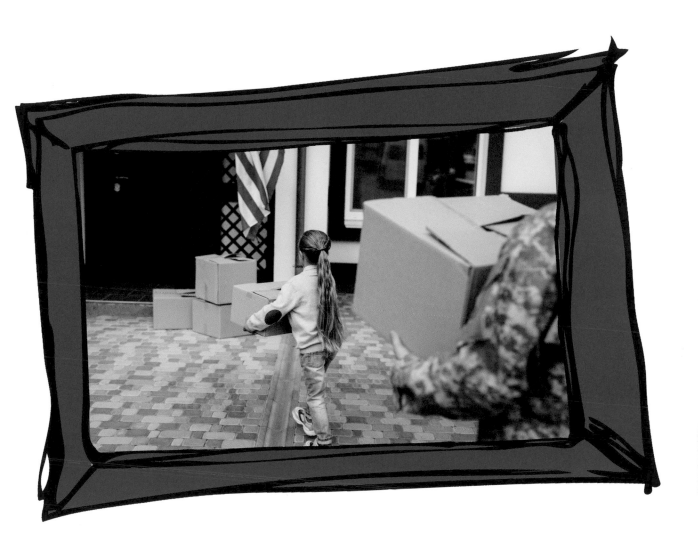

I finished college. I went to the University of New Mexico. Four days later, I had my daughter. I was a single mother.

I started a salsa business.
I worked a lot. But sometimes it
wasn't enough. Friends, family,
and the government helped us.

Who do you help?

I went to law school. I wanted to help my community.

I ran for **office** in New Mexico but lost. But that didn't stop me.

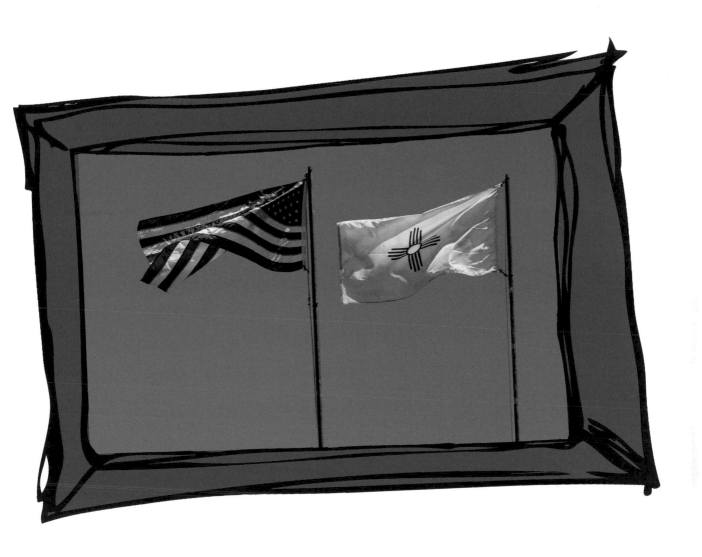

I ran for U.S. **Congress** and won! I am one of the first Indigenous women to win. I fight for nature and Indigenous people.

How do you stand up for others?

President Joe Biden gave me a job in the **presidential cabinet**. I am the first Indigenous person to hold this job.

I will always fight for the people. I will fight for the land. We only have one Earth. Let's take care of it.

What would you like to ask me?

1994

1960

Born
1960

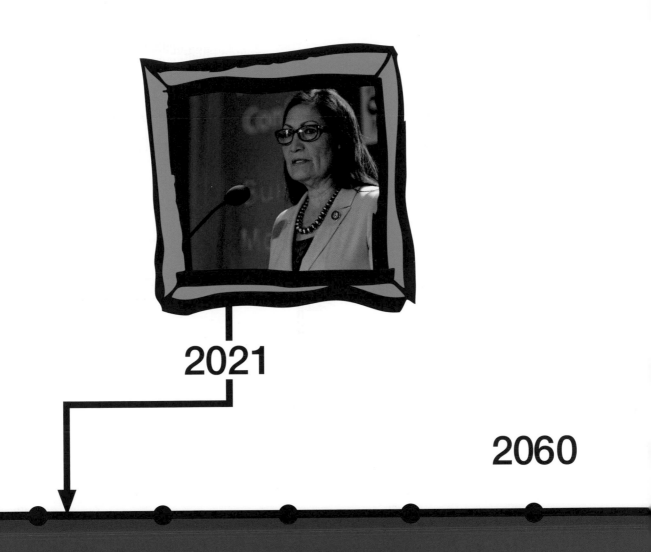

2021

2060

glossary

Congress (KAHN-gruhss) the U.S. government branch that makes laws

Indigenous (in-DIH-juh-nuhss) born or occurring naturally in a particular place; native

Laguna Pueblo (luh-GOO-nuh PWEH-bloh) Indigenous people native to west-central New Mexico

military (MIH-luh-tuhr-ee) the armed forces of a countr

office (AW-fuhss) an important or powerful position in government

presidential cabinet (prez-ee-DEN-shuhl KAB-uh-net) group of people who work with and advise the U.S. president

index

Arizona, 4

community, 12

help, 10, 11, 12

Indigenous, 4, 16, 18

Laguna Pueblo, 4
law school, 12

military, 6

New Mexico, 4, 8, 14

President Joe Biden, 18

salsa, 10

U.S. Congress, 16